REEL MARKETING

The Art of Casino Branding

Julia Carcamo

To my mom and dad who always believed I could do anything, even when they didn't understand this world of casino marketing and branding that I love so much.

CONTENTS

PREFACE

I have been lucky enough to work in casino branding for nearly 20 years. In that time, I have endeavored to share insights and tips through my work, through my Casinos, Brand and More blog, and a variety of publications - *Biz New Orleans, Casino Journal, GGB Magazine, and MS Gaming News.* This compilation of many columns has been organized under the umbrella of Jules Rules - my five pillars for successful branding.

Jules Rules of Branding

Over the years, I have had the opportunity to discuss branding with several executives and marketers. I have seen the usual checklist.

- Start with why
- Research your target audience
- Develop your positioning
- Create your brand identity
- Develop your online and offline messaging

This is a great checklist, and indeed, one that should be considered. Also, I agree that you have to start with your strategy (your why).

I have had great opportunities to polish old brands and create some new ones in my career. I have found that, no matter what the project, market, or budget, to be successful and brand for the long-run, the steps are the same. They are what one of my former agency partners coined the "Jules Rules" of Branding. Developed over 10 years ago, I am happy to say they have adjusted to many market shifts but still hold up.

Jules Rules #1: Know Your Audience/Target/Market

Formal research unearths a great deal of insight. I also highly recommend spending time where your guests experience your brand. Today's consumers are making decisions through the use of multiple channels. Understanding their needs and (perhaps unspoken) desires is critical to developing the brand that will resonate with them. It is at this point that you should consider the various categories of guests you have or want to have. A generic approach to your guest classification will lead to a generic approach to your brand.

Finally, it is time to hit the floor.

Whether you are a casino operator or the owner of a family-owned retail outlet, take time on your floor. Meet and learn more about your guests. Understand what your front line team members have to face when trying to deliver on your brand promise. If you are working with an agency, this is an excellent opportunity for your agency team to understand your operation. It is incredible what everyone will learn and how that will affect the next steps.

Jules Rules #2: Brands are Built from the Bottom Up

I have been known to use an iceberg image as a long-standing example of what makes a good brand because I feel it is the best way to show your operations team how what they do is perhaps the most essential part of the brand. All of the things that happen below the surface are what makes your brand true (or not) to your guests and your team members.

In Jules Rules #1, we touched on how consumers make decisions as a result of interacting with a multitude of channels. In turn, your guest determines if the decision they made was the right one as a result of multiple interactions with your brand. Whether that be how easy it is to find what they are looking for, or how the cashier treats them at the sale, your brand is continuously sending a message. So, it is crucial that the brand vision influence all of the operations.

The next time you embark on a brand project, look at all of those elements first before giving your agency or graphic artist directions on a name or logo.

Finally, consider how the team member journey mirrors the brand experience.

Jules Rules #3: Operationalize Your Brand

When you cannot see a difference between what you say you do (marketing) and what you actually do (operations), that's when you know you have a truly great brand.

First, you have to build an internal culture. As a leader, you have to demonstrate the brand promise in everything you do. Then, you have to make sure the tools you provide your team members to deliver on the brand are consistent with your vision. If you are going to promise a "family-like" experience, your team members have to feel like they are part of that family first, before they welcome new members.

The process of building a brand requires you to not only set a strategy and positioning but to "operationalize" it. More than a logo on a sign or an advertising campaign, operationalization is about how your brand becomes the culture of the organization. To quote Denise Lee Yohn, "It's about putting your brand to use as a management tool — and getting the most value out of it." In her book, *What Great Brands Do*,[1] she points out, "by limiting the definition of your brand to this external, surface level, you fail to realize its full business value." The brand becomes the driver of decisions because more than just being communicated to team members, they have internalized it. In effect, it allows your brand to come to life and enables you to deliver on the brand promise at every moment of the guest journey. Unfortunately, few companies actively align the brand vision with the vision of the operation. Gallup's 2017 State of the American Workplace report indicates only 22% of U.S. employees strongly agree that their company's leaders have a clear direction for their organization! Why? Because a small group of executives often decides vision and purpose for the brand. This vision is then "pushed" down to the rest of the organization in a variety of ways, from memos to pep rallies. The intention and hope are that it will become adopted. Still, the vision rarely achieves the buy-in we need because we fail to include a significant number of people as we shape the vision, purpose, and direction of the organization.[2]

Jules Rules #4: True Brand Programs Share DNA

Like humans, brands have specific and unique DNA. team members and guests reward brands that are true and consistent with this DNA. It is easy to be tempted by the latest trend, but if it does not fit your brand, the guest experience will feel disjointed, and your team members will not have the ability to deliver on the brand promise. The offerings you feature must feel like they are coming from the same source. You are not shopping center offering every option. You have to be selective and only offer the things that make sense to your brand. To paraphrase Steve Jobs, sometimes what you say "no" to is as important as what you say "yes" to.

Jules Rules #5: Make Your Brand Iconic

Iconic brands are not a flash in the pan nor relegated to the latest and most celebrated status. Iconic brands become symbolic of something more than a mere product.

Apple.

Coca-Cola.

Amazon.

FedEx.

Bellagio.

Hard Rock.

More than the products, these brands stand for particular emotional and psychological associations that drive guests to do business with them. When I was at the Isle of Capri and considering the company's brand strategy, we found gold in a file cabinet (metaphorically speaking). Dusting off the Lady Luck brand, we found she had stood the test of time as perhaps THE most iconic casino brand.

This book is divided into sections, each focused on a Jules Rule. You will find assignments at the end of each chapter that you can try on your own at the end of each section.

INTRODUCTION

Everywhere an Isle

Founded by the "father of riverboat gaming," Isle of Capri was a mid-sized regional gaming company with operations in seven states across the United States and in the UK. The guest experience was as diverse as the geography. The company was built on a thematic Caribbean look and feel that was hugely popular at the time it was launched. With a well-worn theme in place at most locations, the 2007 introduction of the company's fourth brand, "the isle." was expected to give the company a fresh new brand identity, but there were problems ahead.

First, there was confusion between the legacy Isle of Capri and the new "the isle." mainly since the community vernacular was to refer to the Isle of Capri as "the Isle." Additionally, the company launched this new brand in the UK, where Isle of Capri was an unknown. Moreover, behind the scenes, there was concern that the fun communicated through the company advertising was perhaps not matching the experience.

Looking to Another Challenger Brand

Retail giant Target is often credited with reinventing American retailing by winning the hearts and wallets of middle America. In 2008, Target's senior management (like many other teams) watched their business decay as the economy slowed, and Americans curbed their shopping. In 2009, same-store sales started declining, first 3%...then 5%...then 10% and the investment community started questioning the team and the company's structure. However, Target's executives realized the change was in consumer behavior and not necessarily the product.

Isle's senior management team faced a similar dilemma. They too, knew the fundamental problem was not an issue with the product, but with the shrinking availability of leisure dollars.

Target's response was identifying the needs of their shopper persona — their "lady" — and then quickly developed a prototype grocery operation for their stores that was designed to drive traffic, highlighting points of differentiation even in the face of a seemingly "me too strategy" (as Walmart had already launched a similar offering). Target was ultimately able to increase traffic and same-store sales as a result of changing their marketing messaging to reflect the reality of the new economy and offering a better guest experience.

Isle also had a "Lady" of their own in mind and believed they could enhance the guest experience and reinvigorate regional gaming by the reintroduction of the iconic Lady Luck brand as well as fine-tuning its foundational Isle brand.

More Than a New Sign and Logo

The Isle team understood the importance of such an icon as Lady Luck. They knew that she deserved more than a new logo. She deserved a transformation of the experience and that each experience needed to deliver on the promise of "fun, friendly and FANtastic value."

Looking again at best practices outside of the industry, the team saw additional similarities to the Southwest Airlines model - a low-cost provider of great experiences with a focus on guest service, friendly employees, and value. At the start of the economic crisis, Southwest looked at the competitive landscape and made a strategic decision to launch initiatives that would create more value in the mind of the budget-conscious traveler. Unlike their competitors, Southwest chose not to charge hidden fees and to focus on service upgrades such as Business Select and priority security access screening lanes to drive incremental revenue. Southwest is one of the few airline carriers that emerged relatively unscathed through the "Great Recession," remaining mostly profitable in an industry hard hit by the pressure on the economy.

Operationalization of the Brand

Seeing the thought processes and similarities in Target and Southwest solidified the Isle's vision that the revival of the Lady Luck was the right move. When launched in Caruthersville, MO, the brand embodied clearly-defined expectations for guests, team members, and investors - an experience focused on value and fun. Fun was always at the core of the company's ethos. The environment was created to be rich with touchpoints, including two new food and beverage offerings, Otis and Henry's (casual dining) and the Lone Wolf Bar (where the beer is always cold, and the wings are hot). Both were designed to support the Lady Luck positioning of value, as well as comfort, and both were an immediate success with guests. Additionally, the well-operationalized brand allowed the company to realize a pipeline for both internal growth and future acquisitions. Team members fell in love with their Lady, often designing creative ways to bring her to life continuously.

Lady Luck was the right brand at the right time. More importantly, the rebranding was firmly rooted in the operator's strategy to match the experience to the expectation of the guest. Moreover, the brand was fully operationalized to create a new business model with a pipeline of growth for the company.

The rebirth of the Lady Luck brand was rooted in a strong operational and marketing strategy. More than a sign or a logo, it transformed the company.

CHAPTER 1:
KNOW YOUR
AUDIENCE

W hen I first started my business, I thought I would be a great casino marketing consultant. After all, I had spent nearly two decades doing just that. I have worked in group sales, as an advertising coordinator, and more. I have swiped cards for entry into the latest slot tournament. I have announced winners in giveaways. I have registered VIPs as they arrived at invitation-only events. I have installed and moved signs. Heck, I have even loaded in-room amenities before opening the doors to a new casino.

But the projects I worked on in the first years of being a freelance contractor turned my world around. I have had the luck to work with a great event and build their marketing. I have helped an author go the (at the time) non-traditional route of self-publishing a novel. However, the vertical that has surprised me the most has been working with casino vendors looking to grow or enter the industry. They have all had good products and a tremendous amount of passion. Interestingly, the thing some have stumbled with is understanding the industry and nature of an operator's day. In other words, they failed to follow Jules Rules #1: Know Your Audience.

After countless conversations with vendors discussing why (oh why?) their product is not cause to drop everything, I find I have discovered some common threads worth sharing, and although they are from the perspective of the vendor looking into the operation, consider how they apply in a B2C scenario.

Time

Think about everything a casino marketing director has on their plate. Typically, they are responsible for database marketing, the players club, host productivity, special events, promotions, entertainment, and advertising. I once worked with a marketing director who was also in charge of valet! At the end of a long day (into the night), one of the last things they probably want to do is return a cold call (or worse yet, get stuck on a 30-minute call because they absentmindedly answered the phone).

Thirty minutes in your day may seem like nothing, but you could very possibly be the 12th person that day to ask for those 30 minutes. Buyer personas continue to be a growing trend. Smart marketers have been doing this for a while, but for some, this is a new piece of the puzzle.

As casino marketers, we typically view guest profiles in terms of ADT, theo, frequency, or on some other transactional level. Building guest personas are a more detailed way of understanding your target audience (and an excellent way to discard those who are not viable targets). A well-developed persona can give you insight into the type of content your potential guest finds valuable and how they consume that information. Also, personas will help you to identify the best channels for your messages to reach them. Take some time with your team to identify your buyers and build out their personas. A few days now will pay off with more efficient use of your time later.

Creating Brand Personas

Creating your brand personas can make your marketing easier.

Three key phases comprise building a strong brand: strategy, articulation, and deployment. As always, the steps you take before deployment are not only the most important but set a foundation for the brand and the business you are building. However, while the articulation stage can often include an in-depth analysis of the competition and the market, it usually involves only a cursory nod to the guest and the things that both motivate and detract.

We have worked with a few properties to develop work their buyer personas that proved to be both enlightening and somewhat fun. Understanding your guest as more than just a sale or visit pattern can help you fine-tune both your marketing and operation.

Personas can help you know your guest as the multi-layered humans they are, converting them from "guest" to "guest". These "pictures" of your current and potential guests are fictional, generalized representations. They help you understand them better and make it easier for you to tailor marketing efforts to the specific needs, behaviors, and concerns of different groups. As a bonus, they can also aid in operational decisions.

How Personas Help You

If you are wondering why you are not getting enough of the right guests or if you are getting complaints, a lack of clarity about your guests' motivations could be the answer. Likewise, if your marketing seems to be falling on deaf ears, it could be because you do not have a good understanding of the guest. Moreover, understanding the guest at this level can aid in how your casino business expands or contracts.

Well-crafted personas can also be one of the best team member training tools in your arsenal because they can have the effect of aiding in the internalization of the guest – almost like knowing a friend, associate, or family member. When you know a person well enough, you understand how to communicate with them more effectively and efficiently, and you know what motivates them to shop, return, and compliment you to their networks.

When outlining your marketing expectations, it is impossible to have clarity without a defined audience. We specialize in casino marketing. We know casinos attract all sorts of people. However, there will always exist an ideal guest that our clients hope to attract time and time again. Some ideal guests fill specific needs (i.e., Tuesday morning or Saturday nights). It is a habit for us to define the perfect guest by the amount they spend. Still, we must also simultaneously understand that two $100 guests can be quite different in their visitation, how they shop, and how they behave. Still, many marketers continue to market to a broad range in the same way even though advances in printing and media have made it easier to do one-to-one marketing (or something very close to it).

Get to Know Your Guests

Until you undergo a persona building process, you will never truly understand the nuances of your guest base. The process will create documentation that will be useful in tailoring communications (so they resonate) or in determining the overall message, the amenities you showcase, and even in the slot titles you purchase or capital expenses you may choose to explore. A well-crafted buyer persona will shed light on

- How a guest might make decisions,
- What challenges they have to overcome,
- When, where and how they spend their time,
- When they are most prone to visit you,
- The best messages and communications channels to reach them, and more.

Consider how your business decisions, messages, and perhaps your channels might be influenced if you had this sort of knowledge.

Personas Are Not Difficult to Create

If you are a new business or a casino under construction, your persona work will more than likely have to depend on anecdotes and stories of competitor or sister properties. The most useful persona profiles, however, will be based on real guests and existing information rather than on assumptions.

The strongest buyer personas are based on research and insights you gather from your database. More than likely, your company has done research. If you do not have them now, you should get your hands on those reports. If those reports are a little dusty (from sitting on the shelf for more than 3 or 4 years), then start talking to your guests. Whether on the floor or through a simple Survey Monkey, Microsoft Forms, or Google Forms survey, begin asking the questions that will help you get to know your guests a little better than what you see in your weekly reports.

There is also much to be gathered from tools you are already working with — such as Facebook Insights and guest comments, to name two. You can upload a list to Facebook, and thanks to the information Facebook already has, your guest profiles are expanded to include income ranges, spending habits, relationship status, job titles, and more.

Additionally, your CRM systems may have much more information than only the name and address.

Start with the Basics

Start with some basics and then add more detail.

- Existing sales information: What are the KPIs or your preferred way to categorize guests?
- Demographics: Male or female? Age? Children at home or empty-nesters? Where do they live?
- Employment: Job, retired, or independently wealthy? Income range?
- Casino personality (for most of our clients): Life of the party or always complaining and

asking for comps? Prefers to play and go? First in line for every promotion?
- Daily life: What does a day look like from the time they wake until they close their eyes? What is challenging them every day? Who makes the entertainment/leisure decisions in the household? What influences those decisions?
- Values and or fears: What is important to them? What keeps them up at night?
- What we add to their lives: Why are they visiting us? How can we make their visit better or more memorable?
- When do they visit? Can we alter the pattern in any way (add a day or lengthen their stay)?

For more color, you can add common complaints, real quotes, and ideal marketing messages (even if the words are not an exact match to the advertising) and the channels that would reach them most efficiently and effectively.

Finally, I always recommend giving your personas names and faces to make them real to everyone. Please print them and add them to your conference room walls and time clock areas so that your guests are always front and center when you are making decisions and plans.

We have four personas for our consulting business. We call them Mary Marketer, Vic Vendor, Jim GM, and Sally SVP - all named after people I have worked with. Depending on your casino and market, you could have as few as one or two personas, or as many as ten or 20. That does not include negative (or exclusionary) personas. If you are new to personas, start small. You can always develop more personas later if needed.

For most casinos, the Pareto Principal is relatively a given. 80% of our gaming revenue will typically come from 20% of our guests. So, my recommendation is to start with the 20%. Then, start working your way through your segments.

Whenever you get all of this detail down, ask yourself, "why?" or challenge your assumption by asking, "so what?" Avoid the temptation to take everything at face value. You have to look below the surface. You want to understand what makes each person "tick."

Turn a Negative into a Positive

Anti-guest personas or exclusionary personas can also be of value. As we mentioned in the introduction, Steve Jobs felt the projects Apple said no to were as crucial as the ones that received a yes. Understanding who your guest is NOT is as important as knowing you they are. Instead of casting a wide net and using valuable resources, you can focus on the guests that will grow your revenue (and those who will not.)

Remember how Groupon was the latest and greatest? Companies offered "loss leader" offers with dramatic discounts assuming they would drive traffic, and these guests would add more to their shopping carts or orders. The trouble was this was not the case for many early participants. They did not understand the value-based guest was not the right fit for them. The benefit of these personas is to help everyone understand the difference between a lousy fit guest and perhaps merely a demanding guest (who could still be a good fit.)

It is the same for casinos, when we fill a concert, it feels great, but that feeling evaporates if they all leave when the show is over. So, we look for the kind of acts our target personas would respond to.

Repeat and Revisit

With each conference or event, I reevaluate my personas to ensure they are still valid or adjust as needed. As competitors enter our markets or economies start to shift, your personas will need reevaluation. Demographics and spending habits change over time. This is particularly true in industries that look to continuously fill the funnel or add new ways of creating revenue.

The challenge of mature markets, attracting millennial guests, and adding new gaming options such as sports betting make it critical that we fully understand the target guest.

Moreover, as your business grows or adjusts, and as you get to know your guests better and better, personas should be updated. As your operation progresses, you start to understand your guests better: how they respond to marketing or your environment, what enhances their visits, what makes them draw back away from you, and more.

You may even start to notice assumptions you made early on need fine-tuning. There may be new technologies or trends that are impacting the guest which should be incorporated into your personas. You may have gaps in your knowledge. for example, if you seem to be losing revenue at a particular point and do not know why then revisiting your personas my hold the answer.

You may have adjusted your operation since the

development of the personas. Conversely, it may be your competitors who have changed and impacted your guests. Also, you cannot ignore changes in the economy or lifestyle that can shape the challenges and behaviors of your guests. All these should cue you to reevaluate your personas and ensure they are accurate portraits of your target guests.

A Word of Warning

As with many marketing tools, they are only as valuable as the use they have. So, before you start this process, you must understand how the personas will play a role in meeting your goals. For these to be actionable, they must align with your strategy. If your strategy is dependent on growth in a particular segment, start with that one first. If you are going to make changes, you have to understand the guests that are most going to be affected by those changes. Tying your personas into your operating strategy is vital to turning these into useful and usable tools.

Additionally, take some time to outline how these personas play a role in your departments, even those who may see themselves support departments. One technique to doing this is designing engagement scenarios for your personas to prepare your teams to interact with guests in various circumstances.

Ask yourself a few questions to understand whether you are creating useful persona documents.

- Are they based on insight, or have they been created based on the opinions of an internal audience (or worse, an internal audience that never has guest contact)?
- Are they capturing the real-life experiences you are creating or only the ideal scenarios?
- Are you creating a monster one-size-fits-all persona or unique ones for separate guest segments? To be valuable, personas must narrow down the pool of guests. Take a woman, 56 years old in a single household, and consider how different her motivations are from a woman, 56 years old with children at home. Both are Boomers, but both vastly different.
- Are they being shared with all team members, or are they being held only for the eyes of the executive or marketing team?

It is an exciting time for marketers. It is easier than ever to get to know your guests so that you can create the brand experiences and messages they like and want. Building guest personas get us even closer to our guests, but they are only useful if they are USED.

Assignment

Select ONE segment or tier and then build an ideal persona from what you know. Try to include the following.

- Background (job, career path, family, etc.)
- Demographics
- Identifiers (such as demeanor & communication preferences)
- Goals
- Challenges
- What can we do (to help them achieve their goals or overcome their challenges?
- Quotes from guests that fall into this persona (remember you are focusing on JUST ONE)
- Objections (what is your property doing

that causes them to object to visit)

- Marketing Message (what are you telling them regularly)
- Elevator Pitch (what you would like to say to them if you had the opportunity)
- Describe a day-in-the-life of your ideal guest, including where your organization fits in and the value you add to that day. Then, find an image of a person that best personifies that guest.

CHAPTER 2: BRANDS ARE BUILT FROM THE BOTTOM UP

C asino owners (and indeed casino marketers) are still asking whether they should invest in branding. The answer is, "Yes." I say this both as one who earns a modest living creating brands and as someone lucky enough to develop meaningful brands.

Today's marketer has many avenues to build brand awareness, credibility, and sales. Unfortunately, many still cling to old-fashioned thinking when promoting their casinos, relying on advertising rather than engagement, which is why they are asking such a silly question. Bill Chiaravalle and Barbara Findlay Schenck, authors of *Branding for Dummies,* will tell you, "More than any quality – even more than strong financial statements, great management, or terrific product or service ideas – brands are the key to winning long-term growth and success. By building a brand, you cast a strong, clear vision of what you stand for. Without a brand, you blur into a dime-a-dozen, one-seems-just-like-another category called commodities. In a sea of similar choices, branding differentiates and elevates your offering, paving the way for awareness, preference, selection, and profitability."[3]

Build a Brand to Shape How the World Sees You

Your brand is what the world – outside of the four walls of your casino – thinks of you.

Brands tell the world what you stand for with every color, word, and image you use. Effective branding makes you memorable, so guests can easily find you. Let's face it. Today everyone Googles you or asks for recommendations before he or she does business with you. Online or off, your brand and how it is presented matters.

But branding takes time. It takes effort. Creating an engaging brand can assist you in reaching your business's highest potential, but it takes strategy and vision. Thinking that slapping a logo everywhere and calling it a day is the opposite of strategic branding. A properly formed brand gives you dividends over time. The brands you see every day would not be as successful in the absence of a well-thought-out branding strategy.

Build a Brand to Reap Dividends

For a one-off or small operation, branding may seem like an expensive and daunting task, but the result is that you will look like a more significant business. A strong brand will help elevate your business and the resulting revenue. In this way, branding can be of even greater importance for small or mid-size operators.

Nascent industry startups are in a unique position to begin their businesses with a strong brand strategy. Let us look at the legalized marijuana industry that is now exploding across the US as an example. In a state like Louisiana, with only 10 available licenses, you can get away with acting like a commodity for a while, but when faced with multiple competitors in a market like Colorado (with over 500 dispensaries), connecting to a brand and cultivating (pardon the pun) loyal guests will make the difference between long-term success and failure.

Additionally, clients and guests will note that if you care enough to put your best foot forward for your own business, you may care enough to manage their experiences.

Guests that identify with your brand values will be more accepting of higher prices than what they are willing to pay for unbranded offerings or those of your competition. Adding new amenities and locations will be easier if you have implemented an appropriate brand strategy because the brand is recognizable, and guests will immediately understand and accept an inherent set of values.

Build a Brand to Build Loyalty

One of the most significant benefits of branding is guest loyalty. When guests form strong bonds with your brand, your marketing can continue even when you are not actively marketing. We see this every day on social media. Strangers, friends, and family are continually sharing their brand stories.

When guests understand (and like) who you are, they will continue to do business with you. As your brand is reinforced in their lives, they will begin to trust you, maybe even love you. The more they believe you, the more they will spread your vision through referrals, reviews, and word of mouth marketing.

Look at that! Now someone is doing the marketing for you...all because you created a compelling brand narrative.

Clearly articulate your marketing message

Positioning and branding can be potent tools to compete in the marketplace but only through clarity of vision and in full support of the business objectives. Some folks love this step. It feels fun to them. It can be a great creative outlet, but that creativity must be in line with your company strategy. It cannot be something that stands separate and apart from what the business is delivering. The positioning of a value-based company is a great example. How many times have you seen messaging for companies promoting the value they give you for the dollar, only to find cheap products at a low price or good products at the same price you could've gotten online or much closer to your home? I highly recommend implementing some voice of the guest programs to guide this step. Large or small companies can do this in many cost-efficient ways.

Look Inside

Understand the way team members are understanding, engaging with, and delivering on the brand. Try this. Walk up to a team member and ask them why guests spend money with you. How does it compare to your brand positioning and messaging? Go through your team member handbook? Does it look like the messages you are trying to convey to your audience? If there is a disconnect between what team members think about the brand, their experience as team members, and what you are trying to market yourself as you have work to do.

We will talk about team member manuals and internal branding in chapters 3 and 4.

Ask for Input

Unless you are the one and only guest capable of sustaining the business, you must ask for input to get different points of view. Your cashiers and guest service agents may not be a part of your marketing team, per se, but they see and hear everything happening with guests and product offerings. You can make this a fun internal promotion and award great ideas. Give them information about the competition, overall goals, and how you want to position (and why) the business. The beauty of this is that you do not have to use every idea, but if you get one great one, is not it worth combing through 20 not so great ideas? Plus, your team members will become your biggest and best brand ambassadors armed with great insight.

Building a Brand Strategy

During a strategy conversation at the inaugural Casino Marketing Boot Camp, one attendee could not believe how blown away she was. "We've been doing this all wrong," she remarked.

Her realization is widespread. Many confuse strategy with tactics, often using the terms interchangeably. Additionally, because a good majority of any marketer's day involves managing tactics and projects, we can usually get lost in the process and lose sight of the goals we desire.

I like to distinguish strategy from tactics by using a travel analogy. A strategy is a destination, and tactics are how you are going to get there. While your travel plans may change – you may opt for a road trip instead of air travel – your destination doesn't (unless there is a sound reason).

In *The Art of War*, Sun Tzu wrote, "Strategy without tactics is the slowest route to victory. Tactics without strategy is the noise before defeat." Using the travel analogy, if you have a destination but no idea how you are getting there, you will never get there. Conversely, the availability of transportation does not necessarily get you anywhere if you do not have a destination in mind.

So how do you set a destination for your brand?

Think long-term. Think holistically. A strong brand strategy will encompass all parts of the company and should include three core elements: purpose, consistency, and emotion.

Purpose. Why you exist, or your reason for being, must be intentionally expressed. An excellent way to discover your purpose is Simon Sinek's Golden Circle. Almost every company can quickly answer the what of their brand: what they sell or provide in terms of goods and services. Most can also explain how. How do we do what we do differently? For some, it is fast, free delivery. For others, it may be frictionless purchasing (like Zappos). But few are ready to answer why. Why is not about money. Why is about your reason for existence. Non-profits must be able to know this if they are to survive, but for-profit businesses seldom have a fully-expressed purpose.

Consistency. If you look back at your brand and feel like "it is all over the place," then you know why consistency is so important.

In a benchmark study by Demand Metric, 40% of respondents indicated their brands were presented "consistently." On the surface, that is not bad news. Unfortunately, the goal should be a "very consistent" presentation, and only 9% indicated such. Worse is that the vast majority were anywhere from neutral to very inconsistent.[4]

The study further shows those who report that their brands are consistently presented are three to four times more likely to enjoy excellent brand visibility than those in the inconsistent or neutral segments. If brand visibility is a goal, then a consistent presentation is non-negotiable.

An easy tool to implement to aid in gaining consistency is the brand style guide (Chapter 5).

When guardrails are not in place, the brand will veer off course. Inconsistencies do not generally happen to harm, but they can. These shortcuts are often taken in the name of expediency. Brand style guides provide boundaries while also helping to regulate the use of brand iconography and language. When consistency is essential, someone has to take the lead and manage the brand.

Emotion. Consumers buy with their hearts even if they tell you they buy with their wallets. The emotion that connects with consumers has a place in their hearts. Years ago, there was a book that grabbed my attention. *Emotional Branding* by Marc Gobe opened my eyes to the truth in the brand. Branding was not about great creative (though that helps); it was about how we can (and should) connect to consumers. Written in a pre-social media age, it predicted the consumer empowerment that currently exists for all brands.

We all consider ourselves logical beings. We look at the facts, make the proper evaluations, and then act. We make several decisions based on gut instinct or emotion.

Malcolm Gladwell's *Blink* argues that these types of quick gut-level decisions save us time and trouble. The use of emotion guides consumers to make these quick decisions when those emotions resonate with them. It is the emotion that creates a long-term connection between the consumer and the offering. Brands like Apple use emotion to separate their products from the rest. Under Steve Jobs' leadership, Apple recognized that we needed technology, but we desired to be part of a revolution, and so, it was born.

Now You Are Ready to Begin Building Your Brand Strategy.

Consider your business goals as the basis for your brand strategy. For instance, new entries hope to capture new guests (perhaps stealing from competitors) while existing businesses hope to hold on and continue growing. There are two destinations for each of these businesses, and their brand strategies should reflect them.

It is an obvious choice, though a mistake, to leave the brand strategy to the marketing team. But a strong brand strategy cannot happen within the confines of the marketing department. A sound strategy must have internal alignment. That means bringing in the departments that will play a key role: product, operations, HR, R&D, and executive leadership.

Facilitating a workshop to answer critical questions will guide your business and brand toward its goals.

- Short and long-term goals.
- Revenue and growth goals. Whose expectations are you trying to meet?
- Entering new markets? Developing new offerings? Enhancing the current offerings?
- Do you have the right staffing to achieve the goals? How does recruiting impact the goals? Do you have the proper organizational structure?
- How will resource allocation contribute to the achievement of your goals?

Then, understand your target guest, the competition, and the unique selling proposition only you can provide. High growth, high-profit firms have clearly defined targets. Experienced researchers will help you understand the strengths and weaknesses of your brand as well as your competitive set. Appropriate questioning can also uncover risks and identify the language cues your target will respond to.

The next step is to develop your brand positioning and messaging strategy. These three to five sentences will ground your efforts in the reality of your guest's mindset. The positioning will be the promise you make to guests, which will determine how you operate to deliver on that promise day in and day out. But it should also be somewhat aspirational to that you can be continually reaching for your goal. Your message will be the translation of your positioning in the communications channels you include. You must never lose sight that your communications must resonate with team members and stakeholders as well as guests. So, while your positioning is at the core, your message may vary due to the interests of the various stakeholders. Your message strategy must address all relevant audiences.

Brand strategy is about the promise you will make and deliver. When adequately developed and infused into the organization, it will guide the choices the company makes. It is what your company stands for.

Resource, Efficiency and Profitability

Are you looking for a way to bring more to the bottom line? Stop wasting your time and money on efforts that will not get you to the promised land. Having a strong strategic foundation allows you to better focus your budget and staffing by showing you where to invest. You can focus on only the marketing programs that will support the overall brand objectives. Historically, we have been tempted to buy the business through reinvestment. Some erroneously believed that offers made guests loyal to our brands. But the emerging generation cannot be bought so easily. They have a new set of values, and how they give their loyalty is entirely different than the guests we have marketed to for years.

Finally, you have reached the surface of the iceberg known as your brand, and you are ready to solidify your brand name, logo, and all the visual cues.

You are should now be well on your way to developing your marketing plan for the coming year. Keep in mind that your plan will live and breathe so that you can adjust as the market demands, and because you are focused, your adjustments will always line up with your brand foundation.

Assignment

- Facilitate a brand workshop to discuss short and long-term goals for revenue and growth.
- Utilizing your persona from the previous assignment and market knowledge, determine the unique selling proposition only you can provide.

- Next, develop your brand positioning and messaging strategy for all relevant audiences.

CHAPTER 3:
YOU MUST
OPERATIONALIZE
YOUR BRAND

T he process of developing a brand strategy forces you to understand and acknowledge who you are in the marketplace and what position you can occupy to differentiate yourself. For many years, some operators considered themselves to be in a monopolistic position. Sure, they may have been the only ones possessing a gaming license for miles, but were they indeed the ONLY entertainment option? Some quickly learned they needed more than a recognizable logo.

The Story Behind the Ad Campaign

This type of genuine cultural engagement is easily seen in the offices of Airbnb or through the story of Zappos. And, while the casino industry has historically relied on communicating jackpots and easy winning, there is an excellent example of branded cultural engagement on the Las Vegas Strip (and many regional markets.)

With 28 locations and over 77,000 team members, MGM Resorts[5] looked to reposition itself from a casino company to a worldwide entertainment company – a bold move. As the company's chief experience and marketing officer, Lilian Tomovich saw this as an opportunity for the company to transform itself based on what was, in fact, the core DNA of the company: entertainment. Over the years, the company had acquired and developed numerous properties. With those properties came the requisite brand positioning efforts. But the company executives understood the long-term vision could not rely solely on guest-facing communications.

Additionally, they realized they wanted the ability to tell a story to Wall Street AND consumers that could be delivered consistently. That meant team members had to be engaged in a culture that was aligned with the company brand. Team members needed to be equipped and empowered to deliver on the brand promise.

The MGM Resorts team initiated an internal cultural change effort. Using the metaphor of a SHOW, not only reinforced the company's brand identity but also came to represent an acronym for the desired culture. The transformation began with a kick-off summit for the 7000 of the company's leaders, explaining the strategy and showing them how to train in a cascading effort throughout the organization. After eight months, ALL team members were trained through custom sessions spotlighting attitudes and behaviors that were consistent with the desired culture.

An internal communications campaign was launched in conjunction with the initiative that was no less polished and produced as the consumer-facing communications – all designed to generate enthusiasm and reach team members from all angles.

Tomovich found fuel for this transformation in the passion for changing team member focus and through the company's commitment to a continuous conversation regarding the brand-culture connection. It is never an after-thought for the leadership.

When you think about it, we are all in the experience business. We all work very hard to deliver amazing experiences, but sometimes we miss the mark. When that happens, you need a strong brand culture to win back guests.

Companies that are successful in combining their both culture and brand find the two inextricably woven into the entire organization. When describing the culture and the brand, you will notice a single set of values. Leaders will act and consistently make decisions. But, more importantly, the difference between what the company claims in its communications and how team members live out the culture is minimal. The bottom line is that the company has differentiated itself in a way that creates value.

More Than a Logo Discussion

In 2018, Dunkin' Donuts announced they were taking their brand in a fresher, new direction. They were not announcing a rebrand but more of a modernization of the brand. While they recognized the overall feel of the brand needed a bit of a jolt, they left the iconic logo untouched. Instead, they looked to physical assets – signs, cups, and packaging – as canvases to create playful expressions of the brand. If you look at the history of the brand's iconography, you will see that it has not changed much over many years. The font was introduced in the 1970s, followed by the pink and orange colors in the '80s. A coffee cup was added in 2002, and its famous tagline has been in use since 2006. Additional modernization of the brand touches the experience – updating the look of the stores and emphasizing digital ordering.

A closer examination will show that as the logo was adapted to a changing world, so did the operation.

Beyond the Splash

As marketers, we often look on with desire as other brands introduce splashy new approaches, but like most change, we must look internally to understand the root of the challenge. Believe me; it is not a logo problem. First, we need to examine what we are doing FOR the brand rather than what the brand is doing for our company. Smart marketers realize that logos are only the tip of the iceberg.

The most successful brand updates are those that have real changes. The best signal of the change is a refreshed logo, but those changes – logo and experience – have to happen together.

Instead of asking the easy questions – are our brands lagging because of ineffective marketing tactics or are we not advertising enough, as the questions that address the brand's equity rather than awareness. The fact is that guests already know about you. The tougher, but more strategic questions are about demand.

> •   Is the message you are sending out speaking to guest's priorities?
> • Is your product satisfying the needs and desires of your target guests?

Your resources are much better spent on understanding what the guest wants. It is only when you know this that you can make the necessary operational changes, and THEN proceed to more effective communications tactics.

Around the year 2000, Special K disrupted the cereal market. Initially introduced in the 1950s, Special K had long benefited from a strong association with weight loss since the 1980s. Unfortunately, the cereal was described as bland, and there had been no real innovation. Towards the late 90s, Special K began understanding consumer priorities asking consumer-focused questions.

- Does our consumer believe what we say about weight loss?
- How should we deliver our promise to our consumers?
- What makes consumers think about our brand?
- What benefits are our consumers seeking?

The result was a powerful connection with their specific target market of women, 25-45. Asking demand-oriented questions allowed them to understand that consumers were looking for easy solutions to their dieting needs. The framing of their "2-week Challenge" and innovation in flavors and product extensions have led to increased market share and modernization of their brand that was not focused on the logo.

That same year, Harrah's (now a part of Caesars Entertainment) underwent a significant shift in how it approached marketing communications. With over 20 properties (at that time) carrying the Harrah's banner, the company had a national image campaign mixed with countless advertising themes running in the various local markets. There was not a clear message. Starting with input from focus groups around the country, the brand team developed positioning and concepts. Then, they went back and tested again, further identifying executional elements such as voiceover styles, age of talent, and music. The process of establishing the overall brand positioning started in August of 2000 and eventually launched at the national and local levels in March of 2001. The new brand leveraged the emotions associated with playing slots at Harrah's, which were uncovered during the research phase – why visits to Harrah's mattered to guests. Although the brand positioning resulted in a library of new creative elements, it did not lead to a logo change, but rather a consistent application of the mark as well as enhanced importance of the experience which guests craved.

As mentioned in the introduction, the addition to the Isle of Capri portfolio in 2007 was expected by some to change the face of the company. The challenge was that not much else was changing. A new management team put the brakes on the "rebranding" to align the company objectives to a defined strategy – matching asset class, market growth, and competition to the brand. The result was a bifurcated challenger brand strategy focused on experience or value but always based on the fun: Isle and Lady Luck. It was only then that we started changing logos.

A Double-edged Sword

The brand vision is at the beginning of any brand project. It is the heritage and foundation on which you build. Mature brands, however, can often become so rooted in their vision that it becomes difficult to adapt and change with the market. But, you don't need to choose between tradition and change. The key is balancing the two. You must align your brand vision with consumer shifts so that you can remain relevant to your guest.

Has your brand become indistinguishable from the competition TO YOUR GUESTS (rather than in your opinion)?

Is there a disconnect between what the identity and experiences are saying today as opposed to when you originated the brand?

Building Brands – More Than A Logo

Many casinos think building brands begins and

ends with a logo, mostly because they think of themselves as a business and not a brand. To some, a brand is Tide laundry detergent, not my body shop or my restaurant. Most assume branding is for the big boys with big budgets and an enormous appetite for advertising. So, they develop the best logo they can afford, put it on the sign, and open the doors for business.

Branding, however, is essential for casinos of all sizes. In the long run, it can increase the value of the company by creating trust, improving recognition, delivering a clear message, and motivating buyers. The immediate benefit is that it can provide direction for all team members and can make guest acquisition that much easier.

Developing your brand can be a great exercise in genuinely understanding your business.

The process requires you to not only set a strategy and position but to "operationalize" it. Operationalization is about how your brand becomes the culture of the organization. To quote Denise Lee Yohn, "It's about putting your brand to use as a management tool — and getting the most value out of it." Her book, *What Great Brands Do* points out that "by limiting the definition of your brand to this external, surface level, you fail to realize its full business value." [6]

The brand becomes the driver of decisions because more than just being communicated to team members, they have internalized it. In effect, it allows your brand to come to life and enables you to deliver on the brand promise.

Unfortunately, few companies actively align the brand with the operations. Gallup's recent State of the American Workplace report indicates only 22% of U.S. employees strongly agree that their company's leaders have a clear direction for their organization! Why? Because a small group of executives often decides vision and purpose for the brand. The vision is then "pushed" down to the rest of the organization in a variety of ways.[7]

The intention and hope are that it will become adopted, but the vision rarely achieves the buy-in we need because we fail to include a significant number of people as we shape the vision, purpose, and direction of the organization. This is an easy trap to fall into, but just as easy to avoid by bringing key stakeholders and front-line team members into the brand discussion.

Do you think you are done now that you know

your guest, found your voice, designed a great logo, and developed a strategy for operationalizing your brand? "LOL," as my nephew says. Consider your brand a living being that needs to be continually cared for and nurtured.

Operationalization of Your Brand

The interesting thing about the casino industry is how we gamble on capital purchases in an effort to rise above the clutter of the marketplace. The trouble is that we are all pretty much looking at the same products with the same hope they will make a difference. I hope my fellow vendors will forgive me when I say, "They are not going to make a difference." More than likely, your fellow competitors will buy many of the same slot machines and likely implement the same new technology. The good news is that you already have the power to make the difference you need. You may not realize it. It is your brand – not your logo or your ad campaign but leveraging your brand as THE business.

The process of building a brand requires you not only to set a strategy and position but to "operationalize" it. More than a logo on a sign or an advertising campaign, operationalization is about how your brand becomes the culture of the organization.

The Picture of Failure

If you peek into my guest room closet, you will find albums upon albums. My mother loved to take pictures. I do too (though now they are all in the form of digital files living in the cloud, my computer and my iPhone). Kodak was an essential brand in our lives (even before I knew what a brand was). Looking back, it is really easy for some to assume that Kodak failed because it "missed" the digital age. But, did you know that Kodak developed the first digital camera in 1975?

I think the company's ultimate failure was because it focused too much on products and not enough on their brand. They were so narrowly focused on being a film company that they lost sight of the fact that they were in the memory-keeping business. Six years after the development of that first digital camera, the company's internal research predicted that digital would do great harm to the film business. So, the company responded by investing in digital image research and filing over 1000 digital imaging patents, continuously extolling their commitment to engineering excellence and the company's "core competencies." Not once did they adapt to the opportunities by reaffirming the brand's raison d'être: helping guests savor and continue to enjoy emotional experiences, beyond the events themselves, through photographs. By the time they jumped on the digital camera bandwagon, it was loaded with competition chasing a fickle younger consumer. At the same time, the company's core fans continued to be Baby Boomers looking to continue capturing their memories.

Great Brands Operationalize and Succeed

The difference between good brands and great brands can often be readily seen in the margins. Great brands tend to have above-average profit margins within their respective categories. In many ways, the operationalization of your brand can carry you from good to great. Take a look at the various rankings of great brands, and you will find a broad swath of companies that have created a culture around their brands: Zappos, IKEA, Patagonia, and yes, Starbucks.

Great brands like these can even recover from a crisis a little easier because they have built robust branded operations and decision making. Tylenol is a classic example. The brand is built around pain relief, but health underlies everything they do. So, when a few of their bottles were laced with cyanide, Johnson & Johnson immediately issued an enormous recall. The brand ethos served as a guiding light in all their decisions. Although their market share took a short-term hit, they were able to grow back successfully.

Employee retention and productivity are additional benefits of operationalized brands. 37signals, parent of a project collaboration software called Basecamp, has cultivated a distinct culture based on their brand – making collaboration productive and enjoyable. With a small number of employees, they have created such traction around their values and operations that they can be more efficient and effective – lowering the costs of recruiting, retention and motivation while benefiting from a high revenue per employee measurement.

How You Can Operationalize Your Brand

Start on the inside. Operationalized brands cultivate a strong culture of stakeholders to influence everything that is done. Gather a "Brand Trust Group" (my play on brand and brain trust) from the enterprise. This group should be front-line and back of house team members. Through facilitated sessions focused on what is working, you should discuss the organization's strengths and aspirations. You should be able to identify the brand attributes that can become trainable behaviors that can, in turn, reinforce the brand in practice as well as influence future strategy.

When Sam Palmisano took the reins of the beleaguered IBM in 2002, he inherited a company that had lost its cachet and was often viewed as increasingly irrelevant. The easy route would have been for him to overhaul the company's marketing strategies – put a fresh face on the company and its products. Advertising IS the fastest way to get attention, but Palmisano understood the best way to reset the organization and strengthen the brand was through strengthening the culture so that employees could turn the brand promise into breakthrough guest experiences. IBM's process of operationalizing their brand turned the focus from products to people.[8]

Make superior choices grounded in your brand. Do not chase trends that are not suited to your brand. Decide what you will or will not do based on the brand's guiding light so that you will attract guests rather than chase them. By being transparent and consistent about who you are and what you stand for, you will attract the guests that fit your brand.

Sweat the details that will continually enhance the operation.

Patagonia sells high-end outdoor gear and clothing. It started in response to the simple need of the founder but has grown into a global company that has preserved its ideals while growing exponentially, incorporating transparency throughout the supply chain and remaining loyal to the trust guests have with them. One remarkable campaign found them eschewing the wild consumerism of Black Friday. Instead of promoting sales, the retailer encouraged people NOT to purchase new items but to repair their existing belongings. With the hashtag #BetterThanNew and #AntiBlackFriday, Patagonia brought its brand essence of responsible living to the forefront on one of the biggest shopping days of the year.

Continuous improvement through measurement. Identify expectations that can be measured through a balanced scorecard framework that provides financial, guest, operational, and team member metrics. Benchmark at the start and continually analyze throughout the process.

Everyone is Invited to the Operationalization Party

An executive leadership commitment is necessary, but company-wide engagement is a must. The operationalization of the brand cannot be relegated to the marketing department. By the same token, marketing cannot operate in a vacuum creating communications and programs that do not reflect the operation. Adequately operationalized, the brand will shape business objectives as well as direct strategic planning and allocation of resources. It can identify new opportunities as well as those that are not well suited. It will allow your team to focus on the right things and will foster alignment.

Think about the most remarkable brand experience you have been a part of recently. It could be opening a package delivered to your door. It could be visiting LEGOLAND or the SPAM Museum. What made it remarkable? What stood out to you, and why? How do you make your operation extraordinary?

Your Brand Is Your Culture

Advertising and media have become even more crowded than ever before, and as technology continues to evolve and play a more significant part in the lives of consumers, it will become increasingly complex. Now more than ever, brands have to figure out how to stand out and maximize the value of their marketing.

The notion of culture is not something most think about when discussing the brand, but when you think about it, brands are built by so much more than logos and taglines. Likewise, culture involves so much more than perks and parties. And, somehow, strategy becomes the catch-all for everything.

Korn Ferry's Hay Group division has found that the alignment between strategy and culture[9] is more often the exception than the rule. The division's research found 72% of respondents agreed that culture is extremely important to organizational performance. However, only 32% said their culture aligns with their business strategy. Most likely, this disconnect comes from a view that sees company values as affecting only corporate reputation and employee recruitment.

The growing number of articles examining concepts such as brand purpose and brand culture has forced companies to reconsider the impact their respective cultures have on the business as a whole. "Culture is no longer seen as an afterthought when considering the business focus of an organization," said Noah Rabinowitz, senior partner and global head of Hay Group's Leadership Development Practice. "Culture is the X-factor. It's the invisible glue that holds an organization together and ultimately makes the difference between whether an organization is able to succeed in the market or not."

Culture doesn't eat strategy for breakfast. It doesn't eat it for lunch. Culture makes strategy possible. Like two atomic nuclei in a nuclear reaction, "when fused, your culture and brand create an unmistakable, unbreakable source of sustainable power for your business."

– Denise Lee Yohn, What Great Brands Do

In her book *Fusion*, brand strategist Denise Lee Yohn introduced me (along with many brand strategy professionals) to the concept of "fusion." She delves into a different idea of workplace culture – one that is less about benefits and more about creating engaged team members who will work together to produce the results that will be focused on your strategy, ultimately building a great brand.

Yohn notes the lack of brand culture alignment

described in the Korn Ferry research as a chicken-or-the-egg problem.[10] "If business leaders don't see how culture impacts business performance, then they don't operationalize — that is, put into action and use — their core values throughout the business and, therefore, they don't see any definitive results from them." As market saturation has made it increasingly difficult for any one company to sustain product leadership over time and to differentiate its brand on product features or performance alone, a definitive brand identity expressed through superior guest experiences can help build long-term guest relationships and maintain higher profit margins. The opportunity is to move from talking about values to embracing them to drive brand performance. You must operationalize your brand.

Yohn states when culture and brand are completely in sync, alignment is manifested visibly in four primary areas: purpose and values integration, team member experience/guest experience integration, internal brand alignment, and team member brand engagement.

Values Integration

The most important question an organization can ask – and answer – is why it exists. Having a purpose can sustain a company even through very dark times. The notion of a brand purpose seems to have become one of the most current buzz phrases, but with good reason. In our competitive environments, we battle daily for the entertainment dollar. As brands, we need to play an irreplaceable role in the lives of our guests. We must live out that purpose so that guests will not be easily lured away by more deliberate competitors. I have been in the boardrooms of companies that aspire to be leaders in profitability and yet promise exceptional service. These two concepts (business goal vs. brand promise) can become quite disconnected and cause confusion for managers, front-line team members, and, ultimately, guests.

Finding your purpose does not have to be a socially or environmentally-focused exercise (as we see from companies outside of our industry). Your purpose will not necessarily dull your ability to create higher profits. Finding your purpose can be an examination of the foundation of the company, or undergoing the Five Why's exercise, or even the Porras and Collins Random Corporate Serial Killer game which challenges you to consider what would be lost if your company ceased to exist and why it is vital that it thrive.

Once found, codify your company's higher purpose in a statement that describes the impact you want to be made inside and outside of your company.

Team Member and Brand Experience

I believe the most significant opportunity we have is in the integration of team member and guest experiences. When that is done, the part we seem to struggle with the most – creative and graphic expression – becomes much more manageable.

Ultimately, you want to create a brand experience for team members, from the way they are hired to the way they are on-boarded and trained to how they do their jobs and interact with guests and with each other. In essence, "you engage your employees in the way you expect them to engage your customer," says Yohn[11]. You must design the team member experience with the same principles you use to create the guest experience, as well as ensure the workplace embodies your brand attributes.

Internal Brand Alignment

Internal brand alignment is the process of bringing the brand strategy into focus through team member communication, education, and enrollment of your team to refocus efforts on creating positive business results through the delivery of the brand promise to guests at every level of the organization. Properly done, this process and the effect of everyone sharing a common understanding can be contagious. This is a result of clearly articulating the brand positioning to everyone inside the organization and ensuring stakeholders consistently agree on what is "on brand," and conversely, what is not.

It also means that the heart of the house systems are delivering on the brand promise. Let's say your brand is all about fun and entertainment. Your zingy tagline drives this home with every bit of communication. Your internal brand is likewise about fun and entertainment. However, nothing about the employment experience is reflective of that fun. Someone once told me that nothing kills a bad product like great advertising. The same holds true when it comes to the heart of the house and your internal brand. All of the creative signs and meetings will do no good if your team members cannot access the tools they need to do their jobs easily or if their resources are continually breaking down.

Team Member Brand Engagement

People often confuse employee brand engagement with general employee engagement (or commitment to the company or job). Engagement efforts are often a way to make employees feel satisfied with their benefits and environment so that they will be encouraged to do a great job.

Team member engagement generally manifests itself in relationships with co-workers, how they view their jobs and careers, and their participation in work activities. These efforts may vary in success, but unless they are intertwined with the brand values, they will not encourage team members to create the type of guest experiences that will advance the brand.

When team members are engaged with the brand, they will think and act "on brand." Team members become your best brand ambassadors because their belief in the brand promise is deep and emotional. They make decisions by thinking of what is right for the brand in the long-term rather than choosing what will produce short-term results.

Why Your Internal Brand Matters

Every year, companies around the world invest thousands if not millions of dollars in developing their brands. Your budget may or may not be as robust, but whether you spend $10,000 or $100,00, that expenditure impacts your bottom line. It can often represent an opportunity cost to have done something else just as important to some other department. The missing piece could have been right in front of you all along – your INTERNAL brand.

Internal branding is less about a logo and colors and more about a philosophy that will focus team members and your operations. It is centered on the company culture and promises to guests, team members, and partners, creating a passionate army of ambassadors. Although it has a slightly different focus, it is still an integral part of your external branding.

Look around at the companies that are successfully growing. Take Amazon as an example. It is easy to say that Amazon is successful because it offers the easiest way to shop, but some may argue that Amazon succeeds, because at its core, there is a culture of innovation – a single mission focus to deliver an outstanding guest experience. In her book *Fusion*, author Denise Lee Yohn calls this "brand-culture fusion – the full integration and alignment of external brand identity and internal organizational culture."[12] She argues (convincingly) that companies "can unleash great power when you fuse together your organization's two nuclei: your culture — the way the people in your organization behave and the attitudes and beliefs that inform them (i.e., 'the way we do things around here') — and your brand or brand identity — how your organization is understood by guests and other stakeholders."

Many organizations currently operate with the idea of culture being about providing logo items to team members or creating parties and celebrations. But culture is often experienced and seen in many unspoken ways. Too often, these ways do not match up to what we claim our culture to be.

How many of you laud or stress the importance of excellent guest service? Now, how many of you have a formalized training and expectation around what is considered excellence? How many executives attended said training? Or, instead, how many of your executives had meetings or calls that could not be rescheduled? How many did you see sneaking peaks at their smartphones during the training?

What if your brand is about warmth, but communications are always done through emails posted on a bulletin board?

Savvy leaders know a strong brand can deliver results. Savvy leaders know an influential culture can do the same (sometimes even better). How savvy are the leaders that see the nuclear reaction that can come from fusing culture and brand? You will create something that cannot be matched. Competitors will always be able to match WHAT you do but never HOW or WHY you do it.

Additionally, as we look to emerging demographics for the future of our casino operations, it is essential to keep in mind that guests are increasingly choosing to support our casinos based on their values. Deliberately linking your brand to your culture to the values of your guests can give you an advantage over your competitors. And, do not forget the digital platforms that allow team members and guests to report to their circles the good, the bad, and the ugly broken promises of our brands.

So, how can you go about creating an internal brand that will enhance your external one?

In today's connected world, your internal brand is continuously being reflected to guests, and what is going on inside your company can often end up being your brand story. If you have been watching any news outlet in the last few months (heck, days, or hours), you can most certainly appreciate the need for companies to have two things in place: a crisis communications plan and solid internal culture. The connected world we live in demands that what traditionally has lived in the back of the house should be right at home in the spotlight.

As companies, we spend a great deal of time developing our external brands. We research. We test taglines. Sometimes, we even test creative. It is not unusual for major brands to spend more money than we will ever see in our total marketing budgets to develop the right shade of blue for their logo. The fact is you can spend a ton of money developing your external brand and supporting marketing, but in this modern marketing world, WHAT you do is only a part of your story. WHY you do it and HOW you do it is just as important.

Ensuring your team members are as connected to your brand as the advertising team is requires that they understand the intended and actual meaning of the tagline and messages. It means your team members feel connected and understand their part as brand ambassadors.

So, how do you master/launch an internal branding initiative?

Define Your Vision

Embarking on a plan without stepping back to define a strategy is a fool's journey. Having a defined direction and vision will give your team members a sense of purpose that can take them from merely seeing their job as a way to earn a paycheck to contributing to something much bigger.

Get Team Members Involved

Your internal brand is about the team members and not your slogan. It is defined by the people who encounter your guests, day in and day out, at the beginning of their shifts and the end of a long day.

Start by asking team members to answer this question: What does my job mean to me? Prepare to be inundated and enlightened.

Do your team members believe in the promise your advertising is making? Get feedback from team members on their perception of the brand promise you are currently communicating. What are guests saying? What are they saying to guests? Use surveys, focus groups, and open forums – as many channels that can ensure everyone has the chance to voice their opinions. This is not a project for your star performers only.

Give Your Internal Brand an Identity that Mirrors the External Brand

A memorable brand identity is a valuable asset for a company. It makes perfect sense that the internal brand is just as valuable (if not more). An internal brand, given the same attention, will "stick" to your team members and give meaning to the work they do. You must work closely with your human resources team to unearth the shared values and ensure your internal and external brands are in sync.

Launch and Embed Your Internal Brand

At this point, you have researched, you have created, you have analyzed, and you have repaired broken systems. Creating a brand does not happen with the stroke of a pen (or email as it were). Brands become memorable because consumers develop emotional connections. Creating an emotional connection between team members and brands takes the same amount of effort.

To ensure a brand continues to underpin every step team members take in performing their jobs, you must consider a proper launch – a multipronged plan to introduce and explain the internal branding and how it applies to the team members and every touchpoint. Consider town halls and events where team member can experience the meaning behind the brand.

Consider updating touchpoints along the "team member journey" – intranet, paychecks, back of house signage, log-in screens, etc. This is not about merely informing. It is about immersing each employee in this brand in a way that makes your brand something to talk about.

Reinforce

Imagine the disconnect team members feel when you communicate to guests that service and attention are your number one goal, and yet your memo to the call center is about cutting down on call times. Your brand has to be the underpinning of everything you do and say so that it will create a connection for everyone at the company.

Additionally, consider how you communicate to everyone, including your internal audiences. Small things add up to a bigger brand picture. Consider handwritten notes rather than memos or pre-printed materials if your brand is about a personal touch. Know birthdays and important dates or provide appropriate CRM tools to help front-line team members if your brand is based on relationships.

A common failure in internal branding efforts is the lull that comes after the launch. To truly transform the internal culture requires continual attention and reinforcement. Examples of team members living the brand should be spotlighted. You can also create incentives or promotions centered on team members exhibiting the brand values.

Hire with Your Internal Brand in Mind

Unemployment is not what it used to be. Some of us work in markets where the talent pool might be a little on the shallow end. But, if you want to drive a consistent brand message, you must hire for the skills and attitude that will represent your brand. Review your job descriptions and the unwritten qualities that your hiring managers look for. Work together to develop an approach that will get you the person that will live your brand.

Though last in this list, hiring deserves a much higher spot. The success or failure of your company can often rest squarely on the shoulders of your team members. I have had to hire in some markets I had not even heard of before joining the company. I have had to hire table service team members in a market where the only other food service job was fast food. Hiring the right people is easier said than done.

Cultivate your culture to become a talent magnet. Rely on brand expectations as well as job duties. Utilize structured interviewing techniques and scoring, which can emphasize the brand expectations. Gather feedback from others. Convenience store QuikTrip has established a reputation for great hiring, despite the gas station C-store stereotype. Becoming an employee is more than an application submission and a quick background check. The process includes testing for appropriate skills that develop brand habits such as becoming fast and good at the registers. And the rigorous onboarding process ensures the formation of a real team. Some employees say they never realized what being part of a team truly meant until they worked for QuikTrip. Because of this, the team is an integral part of the process.[13]

Invest in your external and internal brand. Team members and the operations ARE the brand touchpoints that can either create synergy or friction with your advertising. If you have the luxury of a "brand management" position, that person should be knowledgeable of the operation. They should work with the operations teams to understand and execute against the brand strategy. And if you cannot execute against the strategy, you might want to rethink it.

Although marketing by committee is a recipe for disaster, I will continue to encourage everyone to stop creating and making brand decisions in the marketing or executive offices alone. If team members are not engaged with the brand, they will miss the opportunity to deliver on the promise and feel like an essential part of something bigger. Effective brand building requires that you start at the bottom of the iceberg. Otherwise, you have an ice cube floating in the water and quickly melted.

Many of us work in very saturated markets where we face competition for that weekly visit every day. A key to distinguishing yourself is to engage your team members and align your operations to create consistent and authentic brand moments.

Lead with the Brand

Recently I heard a statement from a company touting how they distribute portions of the employee manual from time to time as a refresher for everyone. I will admit I rolled my eyes because the question was the latest hot topic in the news. They missed the point that HOW executives behave, and the examples they set, say more than any part of the employee manual. The bottom line is that your leadership needs to set the example if your internal branding efforts are to make any sort of positive impact.

If you still think developing an internal brand is not worth the time, effort, and expense, consider that your team members are meeting and greeting your guests in a variety of ways, in a variety of styles, and through a variety of channels. They are the faces and voices of your brand. Effective internal branding can bring considerable benefits to your bottom line. Companies whose employees understand and are committed to the brand perform better and have higher guest satisfaction, and ultimately, higher shareholder value.

Internal Branding: Does the Inside Match the Outside?

You have spent hours working with focus groups and weeks (if not months) working with your agency to develop your external branding. You have flipped the switch, and everything looks incredible.

Your drop benefitted with a nice little bump. Your campaign may even win you and your agency an award or two.

Fast forward three months, and you are back in the same spot you were 12 months ago. Now what? You could have sworn what you needed was a branding effort to dust off the cobwebs of stale campaigns. More free play? New campaign? New agency? What is missing? For some answers, you may need to look inside.

Does the team member experience reflect your brand?

Do your team members know what your brand even means, and do they feel they have the tools to deliver the promise you are making in your advertising?

External brands typically have a well-defined style guide that will address everything down to the tone of voice and key statements. Internal communications are often left to the creative genius of an admin or employment coordinator. These folks may be very gifted communicators but can lack clear brand direction, resulting in a different look, feel, and tone for every piece of communication. While this may seem fun, your internal communications should reflect the same attention and thought that is given to external communications. The internal and the external must reflect connectivity to assist team members in understanding how the internal and external are related. When you draw on core ideas for both your internal and external communications, it will be easy for team members to see the vision. Furthermore, it will give them a clear vision to influence the decisions they often have to make on the fly.

What makes you, YOU?

The first step must be to define your values and your mission. Without direction, your operation will lack purpose, creating a plethora of wasted resources. Having a clear mission will give your team members a needed sense of purpose. Companies with a sense of purpose have been known to outperform those without one by as much as 400%. A clear understanding of purpose can change a team member's attitude from "I am doing my job and earning my paycheck" to "I am contributing to something I believe in AND getting paid." Define a mission that will make team members want to come to work and do a good – make that great – job.

Engage Everyone

In a void, an internal brand is nothing more than tone-deaf advertising if it is not created and embraced by everyone. So, get everyone involved. Get input and feedback from all areas and layers, starting with front-line team members and up through management. Use focus groups and surveys, discussions, forums and Q&As or "lunch and learn" events in the EDR. When you provide team members with a sense of ownership, they will be receptive to concepts and ensuring success.

Assignment

- Survey team members about the meaning of the brand.
- Identify a brand experience you have had that you could describe as remarkable. How can you create a remarkable experience?
- Assemble a Brand Trust Group for monthly brand reviews.

CHAPTER 4: BRANDED PROGRAMS SHARE DNA

What is the first thing that happens when you start a new job? Usually, someone from HR welcomes you with the employee handbook and a bunch of papers to sign.

The employee manual – the collection of policies and procedures every new team member gets when they start a job. It is thought to be a critical document for setting clear expectations: what to wear (or not), how to behave (or not), and how to earn and use your time off. Organizations put much time, effort, and care into crafting this tome of rules.

Depending on where you work, the employee manual could be one card or a book rivaling *War and Peace*. The number of pages is not proof of the value of the writing to your company even if you took weeks and months putting it together, getting it past legal and proofers. Why? Because it is often missing an exploration of one of the most critical pieces of content that will help your team members grow your business.

What is this resource? Brand insight and how they, as brand ambassadors, fit into it. YES, your team members can do more than their jobs. They can be the key to improving your business if armed with the resources they need.

If the purpose of the team member manual is to create a sense of stability and avoid failure, you must do more than welcome team members with a dress code. To improve your culture and increase productivity, team members must be invested in your brand. You must create and maintain a culture that is inextricably tied to your brand so that how it is perceived on the outside matches the experience on the inside.

To do this, you need first to understand your core values and your brand purpose. These will help guide the overall development of an innovative team member manual, both in how it is created and communicated and perhaps even in how it is delivered.

Then, you must understand the purpose of the team member manual. If, indeed, it is only to contain the behavior of team members, you can stop reading now. This section will be of no interest to you. If, however, the purpose of this exercise is to build a strong foundation that inspires your team members to create brand experiences that your guests will want time and time again, then you want this document to be so much more than the usual.

Assess the Existing Alignment of Your Stated Mission and Your Brand Purpose

While many manuals include a company mission statement, it can often appear reduced down to an elevator speech. Alternatively, worse, it could be a dream from many years ago that has changed and morphed due to ongoing operations and may no longer be valid or useful. As I advised at the beginning of this book, you must ask and answer specific questions that describe your organization in ways it is known today, what it should be doing, as well as how everyone thinks and behaves. How do you have to operate and work together differently to achieve the purpose? What must you start doing (or stop doing) to make your brand values a core part of how you do business?

Adopt a Single Vision for the Organization

Rather than relying on a typical corporate mission statement – which is usually focused on the company's goals – describe your mission as a brand essence statement and the purpose or role the brand plays in the life of the guest. As guests are faced with ever-growing options for their entertainment dollars, your brand must play an irreplaceable role in their lives. A brand purpose statement helps to set and maintain a singular focus for team members.

Adopting this single vision can be tricky for some, but it does not have to be. Most casinos adopt a mission or purpose that outlines what the company does, produces or sells, and then sets a goal to achieve some target (typically financial). Then, they go about establishing a brand purpose – or what they want to be known for. Your purpose, however, should be seamlessly integrated as one. Traditionalists separate a company's mission (the reason for being), vision (the desired future) and mission (how it goes about fulfilling the vision), but they do not have to be three different statements. A simple yet clear purpose statement can engage even the most skeptical or apathetic team members by making their work meaningful.

Express Your Singular and Unique Brand Values and Purpose

It is not unusual for companies to adopt a set of behaviors and values to internally guide decisions and team member actions and then a separate set of values and practices for the guest experience. An example I typically point to is the company that wants to be industry-leading in profitability yet promises as a brand to be generous in service. This sort of incongruence can confuse at best and create team member turmoil at worst. Bridging these two and creating a core set of values will resonate with team members and create an alignment of the view of the brand that anyone can follow. Valve's employee manual has set a standard for walking employees through the WHAT of the brand - so much so that it went viral a few years ago. It is a great example to look at.

Focus on the Expectation and Not on Platitudes

Years ago, a wise man taught me the concept of "developer speak." He said that operators who do not have unique experiences to sell rely on the things that make up their product – 800 thread count sheet and luxurious soaking tubs. Are you starting to get the picture? Are you using meaningful language in your team member manual? Because team member manuals are traditionally one of the first documents given to new hires, the brand voice and values should be introduced if it has not been through the recruitment process. Additionally, because so many team member manuals can often feel the same, the language you use can be an opportunity to create a distinct impression in the mind of team members.

Develop Mindsets and Behaviors That Will Guide Team Members to Create On-Brand Guest Experiences

Nordstrom's one page, one simple rule employee manual is a single card, yet one of the best examples of what we typically understand to be an employee manual. One side reads, "Our number one goal is to provide outstanding guest service. Set both your personal and professional goals high. We have great confidence in your ability to achieve them, so our employee handbook is very simple. We have only one rule…" The other side? "Our One Rule. Use good judgment in all situations. Please feel free to ask your department manager, store manager, or Human Resources any questions at any time." With this simple, almost non-existent employee manual, Nordstrom puts the focus on the employee's role in creating and growing the brand.

Get More People Involved

Most team member manuals are created within the human resources department with little to no assistance from marketing. If your goal is for all team members to understand the brand purpose and truly live the brand, you should consider getting involved in more than just a layout and design capacity. Launch and distribution are marketing specialties and could create a memorable brand experience for team members. This partnership could also create new avenues for the way the manual and its contents become a part of the day-to-day culture. Technology has opened up multiple platforms for creating, hosting, and distributing team member information such as video, slide shows, even cartoon illustrations that entertain and teach proper brand behaviors.

Walk the Walk

There are some great examples of company employee manuals that are indeed a reflection of the brand. Tech company Trello uses its platform to deliver its manual to employees. Even the first entry is a nod to their brand: *Dust off the age-old employee manual for today's modern workforce.* Hubspot's employee manual also warrants a mention because it manages to communicate a great deal through a simple PowerPoint, publicly-posted to SlideShare and further cementing their commitment to transparency – a principal brand value.

Most casino marketers will have spent little more than reading time with an team member manual. However, designing one that is not only useful, but purposeful is ultimately worthwhile. Your employee manual can and should be an extension of your brand materials. So, I encourage all of you to take a look at your current manual and evaluate how it is assisting employees in creating the brand experiences that are necessary to grow your operation. A human resources/marketing partnership is key to building and empowering brand ambassadors.

What to Do with Brand Acquisitions

Your company has announced a new brand acquisition, and up until now, it has been a competing brand.

First off, this really should not come as much of a surprise. According to a BizBuySell's survey, over 500,000 businesses change hands each year, and the gaming industry is no stranger to this type of action.[14] Consolidations and mergers are a constant source of discussion in the casino industry.

So, let's say the above happens. As executives in charge of marketing for your property or company, what is your next step? Indeed, the list of compelling questions coming from a merger with competitors and non-competitors are numerous. What is the regulatory impact? What is the impact on the guest? How will we integrate systems and policies? What happens to the existing brands?

Let's look at the question of the brands. With every consolidation, there is a chance companies will acquire brands that are entirely different from their existing core. Some may be stronger than the ones they started with, and some may be much weaker. How do you decide which ones to keep, which ones to transition, and which ones to polish a bit? And, how do you handle consolidation of efforts when you have a portfolio of numerous brands?

To start on a positive note, buying an existing brand helps you skip all the steps to building a new brand and the costs associated with creating and launching something novel. If the casino you are buying has trademarked slogans and elements that resonate with the guest, you have already covered a time consuming legal process. And if those trademarks resonate on a national scale, then you have something that could strengthen your existing operations.

But even if this is the case, at some point, you will have to come up with a unified and integrated brand marketing strategy for the entire portfolio. Here is some advice on how to make this process as painless as possible.

Establish a corporate DNA. A successful portfolio integration will indeed share DNA, but to first understand this, you must define the company vision — your corporate DNA. This necessary step will help determine if a new brand can be easily integrated. This could also open your eyes to leveraging a brand you had thought of as a strong contender before this examination.

There are some casino brands in our industry that have already established easily recognizable public personas — the data-driven company, the fun and friendly one, the one creating great resort getaways. Take an (honest) look at your company. What is your mission? How are the brands focused on the mission? Better yet, ask your guests what they think you are trying to accomplish and how well you are doing that.

It is also a great idea to get an outside point of view on your brands and your mission. As owners of these great brands, we can often fall in love with the concepts we create and lose sight of reality. Additionally, over time, the brands shift, often becoming something altogether different than what we initially envisioned, a phenomenon that someone outside the branding team will be more likely to catch.

Your agency should be a key part of the team, not only because they will take the journey with you but because their daily efforts expose them to brands in and out of the gaming industry. The insights gleaned are an advantage to us as brand managers.

Create Categories that Promise a Distinctive Experience

Take a good hard look at your brands. Speak to guests and get your hands on some in-industry and comparative industry insights. Now, you can start to understand the precise categories of experiences and begin to develop a clear vision for your brand portfolio.

Consider the Marriott acquisition of Starwood Hotels & Resorts portfolio in 2016. Marriott had to understand the categories of brands they had as a new company: luxury, upscale, and so forth. They had to ask questions of how well utilized the brands were and how well known they were to understand which brands they would move forward with.

Le Meridien was a brand with an international name but had been somewhat underutilized. Was it worth keeping and expanding, or would they change the flag to something like Renaissance, which Marriott was building as its upper-upscale brand? The questions you ask about your brands will determine which you keep, which you change, which you update or modify and which will be put away in the legal files for some future use.

Don't Break Any Hearts

You must always be mindful of the team members that have worked hard to bring the brands to life before your entry onto the scene. There was a time when companies would acquire ongoing operations and instantly deem them "our brand" without understanding the heart and soul that kept the brand alive enough to become attractive for purchase—the team members.

Additionally, as the heart and soul of the brands, these team members can give it life or let it wither and die. When the corporate marketing team at Isle of Capri thought of dusting off the Lady Luck brand, the initial reaction from the general managers was dubious at best. The most common comment was, "we got rid of that a long time ago," as if to ask, "why would you do that?" Then, something started to happen. The energy shifted as some started remembering what a great experience it had been. Quite frankly, no one could remember why it had been put away with the legal documents.

I never asked why the previous team chose to get rid of something that seemed to be working because I know what it is like to be in love with your brand to the point where you think the only option is to rebrand an acquisition to the one you know like your own name.

Once you start the transition, keep in mind this is not merely a logo swapping exercise.

Nor is it a license to put a logo on everything that does not move fast enough to get out of the way. Remember the team members. This is not about handbooks and training sessions. Tell them the brand stories that will become lore on your gaming floor. Then let your casino properties start to breathe on their own and figure out how to live it at the local level.

I cannot stress this enough. One of the biggest mistakes I see is thinking it is about colors, logos, and slogans. You must stay focused on the experience, day in and day out, and discover how to deliver that experience consistently.

A final consideration I want to point out is about the brands that are going to be woven through and across differing experiences, like your buffet brand or your players card. These rebrands are often considered obvious steps, but you have to think about how those brands may differ by location. If you do not understand those nuances, you will quickly find you have one brand that has a variety of different meanings because of the operations themselves are different.

Deciding what to do with a new portfolio of brands says a lot about the company and its vision for its stakeholders. It only seems right that this process is well-thought and appropriately executed.

Assignment

- Review your recruitment and on-boarding processes and evaluate how they are assisting team members in creating the brand experiences that are necessary to grow your casino operation.
- Consider how you would approach any future acquisitions. What are the parts of the DNA that need to be present in order for the operations to thrive?

CHAPTER 5:
MAKE YOUR
BRAND ICONIC

W e have finally reached the top of the brand iceberg - the surface manifestations that make your brand recognizable.

Naming Your Brand

Whether you are building a new casino company from the ground up or creating a new product or service for your existing casino to market, the naming part can be quite a challenge. It has to sound good when it is said aloud, and it should be easy to say and spell. It should be specific enough for the consumer to get a sense of the experience you are creating. And above all, it needs to sound appealing. As an example, the next time you open a menu and consider the appealing Chilean Sea Bass consider how tasty it would seem if it were listed by its actual name, Patagonian toothfish.

As casino marketers and creative business leaders, those necessary qualities that I just mentioned are not too hard to work with. My legal friends will hate me when I tell you this, but the thing that tends to bring creating a name to a screeching halt is often the legal aspect of the name itself – the trademark.

Google is Only a First Step

I used to work with a creative genius who would Google a name whenever we were brainstorming new brand names. If he did not find a website bearing the name, he thought we were good to go. Nope! A web search is a good start but only a start. You have to consider businesses that may not have a website (shocking, I know). Sometimes, he would find a site and determine the name was not being used the same way. Let's say you want to name a nightclub and there is a coffee house across the country with the same name. Can you use that name? Probably not depending on how the coffee-house registered their trademark. This is where your lawyers come in very handy!

The other thing my creative friend used to do is attempt to overcome a trademark concern by changing spelling or using a translation of an existing trademark. That is also a problem.

As you go through your brainstorming process, use the U.S. Patent and Trademark Office's trademark search tool. It is quite easy to use and will allow you to see if the name you want, including similar and variants of it, are in use. Then look for the domain availability. Ideally, the domain is somewhat keyword focused. You should also do a social media search to ensure you can build a consistent identity across all of your communications.

Call a Lawyer

Once you select a name, you should ensure it is properly registered and protected. This can be somewhat confusing if you are new to the naming game, but although it can be done on your own with a modest investment of time and money. However, a lawyer specializing in intellectual property can be a lifesaver. They can assist you in registering your most valuable assets: the words, names, symbols, and logos that distinguish you from everyone else. They look for the opportunity to protect you in more ways than are apparent to the inexperienced. This can be a massive help if you operate in a competitive industry, and I think we all agree the casino industry is highly competitive.

If you are committed to using a name that is already in use, you can consider a licensing agreement with the holder of the trademark. This agreement permits you to use the mark. Licenses can vary in terms but should include specific identification of the mark as well as any restrictions and expectations.

Keep an Eye on Your Name

Once you have gone through the long process of determining and trademarking your brand name, you must monitor it on an ongoing basis. Not everyone will go through the same careful steps you did. If you find someone using your trademark, often showing proof that you have trademarked the element will be enough to convince them to cease. If they do not stop, you may want to go a bit further by possibly assessing any damages and then taking some level of legal action.

The right name can make the difference in propelling you to success because it can provide a mental shortcut for your target guests. It is essential to spend the appropriate amount of time to ensure you can use it and that no one else is using it without your consent.

Designing Your Identity

There are several articles, books and resources specifically focused on the design of logos.

Logos have a tremendous effect on what a consumer thinks of your brand. It is overwhelming to think about how much work this image must do. Indeed, a picture IS worth a thousand words. How we see and react to logos might just be the precursor to dating apps. Logos are typically the first impression your brand will make.

Check out the competition. Although you do not want to replicate what your completion is doing, you want to make sure you stand apart so that you are recognized as the obvious choice.

You want it to communicate who you are and what you are. The design style you opt for will be a reliable indicator of your brand — modern and sleek, playful and fun, solid as a rock. Your brand essence will point you in the right direction for the type of logo that will best represent you.

Types of logos

There are a variety of styles you can use to design your logo. The most common are abstract, pictorial, emblems, and typographic.

- Abstract logos use subtle placement or images to create a message such as the FedEx hidden arrow. As the brands mature, you may start seeing the hidden element come to life as a shorthand for the brand identity.
- Pictorial logos will feature an image like the Apple apple. When combined with other elements, some of these logos can create underlying meaning to the words.
- Emblems immediately give the reader a sense of tradition; they are typically very intricately designed.
- Typographic logos take simple (or artistic) fonts to another level by combining the forms in ways uniquely identifiable to the brand.

Test. Test. Test your logo options with potential stakeholders and across a variety of execution to ensure no application overpowers your brand meaning and that it remains appealing to your targets.

Logo Makeovers

Look around at the brands that have stood the test of time. If you look closely, you will see that successful ones have found a way to adapt to the modern world — whether that be digital applications of their identities, adapting to changing consumer lifestyles and needs, or finding better ways to build a mousetrap.

Historic identities that are still viable today will have invariably found a way to integrate the equity earned from their original logos with the visuals that dominate our lives today. In some cases, this has been a thoughtful, well-crafted evolution. For some, it has been in response to the current communications landscape that requires our brand identities to live in a variety of digital (and small) mediums. And sometimes, modernization of a logo has been a direct result of simple design tools that have allowed designers to create logos with real stopping power. Regardless of the love you have for your logo, its life will always be informed by the norms, trends, and standards of the day.

A Makeover, not Plastic Surgery

Your logo might be ready for just a tiny bit of help — a refresh. A logo update is like a personal makeover that transforms how a person, or brand, is perceived. The foundation (much like your bone structure) does not change, but the new clothes and makeup are updated and designed for today. The truth is no logo can stay relevant forever if it does not keep up with changing guest sensibilities.

Ask yourself a few questions:

> • When was the last time your logos were updated? Are they showing signs of aging?
> • Is your logo too complicated for today's digital channels?
> • Is your company evolving? Are your guests changing?

If any of your answers have you looking at your logos with a new eye, there are a few basic approaches to modernizing your logo, which can be relatively pain-free, if not committee-free. Keep the logo but update the tone to match a strategy.

> • Add messages (such as tagline) or re-evaluate a hierarchy of graphic elements
> • Freshen or expand the color palette
> • Simplify or remove complex elements (particularly those that cannot translate

on digital platforms).

When Waste Management updated its identity with the color green, it was because they were focusing on becoming a green, responsible company, and they had recently started communicating the proof of their environmental efforts.

The Miami Dolphins have updated their logo over the years while still honoring the legacy and equities of the brand. There is still a dolphin (though admittedly a less "goofy" version), and the warm Miami sun. The palette is basically the same but brightened a bit. More importantly, a simplified design gives them better usage in digital and video. The evolution of the mark has focused on what continues to be important and what can be thrown away.

As marketers, we have all seen cases where logo updates or changes have been received with some level of negative feedback. You should anticipate some level of negativity. Prepare your executive team and find an agreement as to which audiences (and opinions) truly matter to your brand. If possible, do a little research before you roll out a new look to a beloved brandmark. Otherwise, you may end up like Gap and reversing your decision with no real rationale.

A strategy must drive any changes.

The Brand Style Guide

It is no surprise that we all use the same words and phrases but often with different meanings. One example is "brand guide" or "style guide" or even "brand style guide." This was painfully evident to me recently when we provided an estimate for a brand guide, and the recipient responded, "This price seems excessive. The design resources are usually too busy to refer to a style guide." I was speechless and mildly insulted, but I then realized what I thought of as the brand guide was quite different than what the client had envisioned.

I think I have banged my drum enough to hope we can all agree that a brand is more than just a logo. Your brand is how and what your guests and target audiences think and feel when they see or hear your name, your communications, and your stories. It comes across in your tone, manner, images, and interactions. A properly formed brand style guide makes the brand understandable to all and influences actions, so that the brand can come to life at all touchpoints. Remember Jules Rules #2 says a brand is built from the bottom up. And at the very bottom is your brand style guide.

Why a Brand Style Guide is Necessary

A logo style guide is essential to create a robust framework and starting point for your brand's visual identity. As the graphic expression of your brand, you want to ensure consistency as well as correct usage. That consistency is only ONE essential part of building a brand that will build awareness over time. But, you also want to build trust with that awareness. That is where all of those branded touchpoints come in.

Brand style guides (BSGs) will support your initiatives by ensuring actions are relevant to the brand's goals and vision. Programs based on the BSG will help separate you from your competition in a way only you can own. When adequately leveraged across the casino, your BSG will not only influence your consumer messages; it will determine the way you speak to team members, the investment community, and the community at large. The brand will influence your future and current team members and their perceptions of how you treat team members and candidates.

What to Include in Your BSG

Robust, useful BSGs will include all of the following and maybe even more.

- Brand essence and positioning statement
- Brand history, if available
- Brand architecture, if applicable
- Logo specifications such as colors for print and web, as well as any secondary logos, wordmarks, or monograms
- Colors can vary by production process and devices. To ensure consistency, you should specify values for each usage. Include primary, secondary and tertiary colors, limited and single-color versions of the logo (of particular importance when producing promotional items), Pantone, CMYK, RGB and hex colors.
- Logo placement and size specifications, both minimum and in relation to other assets with examples showing both how to use and how not to use the logo
- Taglines and their usage
- Any visual cues that are integral to the brand's visual identity, such as icons, calls to action, and treatments.
- Photography style and composition
- Fonts should be a part of the style guide, along with their weights, usage, and al-

ternative web-safe options. Additionally, there should be direction on how elements, such as titles and headlines, body copy, and legal disclaimers, should be styled.

· Digital and web-safe specifications, such as fonts, buttons, elements, and icons

· Voice and tone of writing, including keywords and style, as well as what your brand never says. Consumers will personify brands as if they were real people. So, the tone that you are using across your marketing and touchpoints will further bring that personality to life.

· Standardization of dates and times.

· Asset libraries, such as images and trademarks.

· Examples of correct and incorrect usage for each element.

Great BSGs will become a living guidebook for the brand, growing and adjusting to market, media, and consumer changes.

A comprehensive brand style guide will define the company's language and visual image to ensure a consistent tone through all communications. Additionally, it will drive a cohesive guest experience to nurture trust and loyalty over time for both current and future guests.

The Sound of Your Brand

If you were asked to describe your brand voice, what would you say? How would you explain how you speak to your guests and your team members?

Let's try this approach. What if your brand were a person standing next to you at a cocktail party? You are chatting. Later, someone says, "Hey, who was that you were talking to over there?" How do you describe them (your brand)? I use this exercise because I have come to realize that the notion of brand voice is not as well known among some marketers as I previously thought. More often than not, I have gotten the name of a brand's voice over talent when I have asked about the brand voice. True story, but this is not voice-shaming. This is about my realization that some of us still struggle with voice. Can you close your eyes and hear your brand?

Coke vs. Pepsi

Mercedes Benz vs. Chevy

These brands evoke iconic images but close your eyes and listen to one of their ads. Without hearing the name, you would probably know who it is. They are distinctive and consistent in their brand voices, and they are leaders in their categories. Coincidence?

A brand's voice helps guests "feel" the brand whenever it communicates. A brand voice humanizes the brand for the consumer, making it easier to relate and connect to it based on shared values.

Today's dominating use of social media has allowed even the smallest and newest brands to establish unique brand voices. Squatty Potty took the social world by storm with its unique videos — a mix of eye-catching visuals and humor that focus on connecting and entertaining rather than selling.

Tasty's humanity has opened many doors for a relatively new brand. Oreo's famous dunk in the dark tweet during the 2013 Super Bowl was a first step into what has become a very recognizable brand voice. Wendy's snarky attitude, though often at odds with its non-digital branding, is another.

Cultivating and maintaining a strong brand voice requires a mix of understanding and policing, but first, it requires that you understand what your brand stands for (and what it does not.)

A brand's voice needs to flow from the vision and mission of the organization to the smallest details.

There must be commitment so that the voice does not falter in the rush of real-time responses or last-minute programs.

So, how do you set and maintain a voice for your brand?

Often the brand name can indicate a voice. Think of Squatty Potty as playful or the pragmatism of PayPal and the emotional tone of Triumph Motorcycles.

Is your brand helpful? Is it funny? Is it transparent and honest? Professional? Hip? These are the types of brand values questions that must be asked and answered to set your tone. Understanding the brand values and tone allow you to select the language – or keywords – that will represent the values of your brand and communicate your message consistently and effectively. Included in this process is also understanding the type of language you want to avoid. With time these key phrases and words become a natural part of your communications

Consistency is key. Remember that cocktail party I mentioned? Imagine that person you were chatting with after a few too many drinks. They come up to you and whoa! This is not the same person at all! That is EXACTLY what happens when guests get mixed messages. One ad shows your professionalism, and the other is snarky. That will leave anyone wondering who they are doing business with and why they are considering handing over their hard-earned money.

Most casinos have more than one guest (or persona), and although their needs and motivations may differ, good marketers must understand that the brand is one serving many, not many serving many.

Additionally, casinos will have more than one person to be the touchpoint with the guest. All team members and representatives must be properly trained on the brand values and voice. This will provide the confidence they need to ensure on-brand interactions. The addition of social media also makes it important that any training address the difference between personal and brand voice. Every word and image shared will add or detract from the voice. Consistency will protect your brand from having minor slip-ups become significant issues, and the bonds you form with followers will become stronger.

Sprout Social recommends a few exercises, including storyboarding your voice as a writer would develop a character. What does your brand like? What does it dislike? What does your brand want to be? What sorts of colloquialisms does your brand use? Thinking of your brand as a human can give you great insights.

Mood and Medium

Although consistency is vital, it is not concrete. Understanding the mood and medium of your message can guide you in the application of your voice. For example, loyalty programs often hit a reset period where the past visit and spend levels determine the benefits a guest will receive for the next period. If the guest is getting more in the next period, it is a no-brainer, but what happens when you are the fun, friendly brand, and you have to tell a guest they are getting downgraded? A strong understanding of the brand's voice will make this an easier process.

Different mediums (or channels) also require a different approach to your brand voice. The most obvious contrast is social media versus direct mail. One has to be quick and to the point, while not disengaging the audience. The other gives you much more opportunity to walk the reader through the message. Although the approach may differ, the voice should not.

Assignment

- Introduce your brand to that person at the cocktail party. Try to describe it as humanly as possible.
- Create a brand style guide that goes beyond graphic standards. This should include your brand mission, vision and values statements, as well as what your brand will and will not do.
- Create a list of keywords and phrases that are, and are not, in your brand lexicon and include them in your style guide.
- Standardize your fonts, colors, and images. They are as important as the tone, manner, and words you use.

Lagniappe - Pronounced LAN-yap.
Defined as a little something extra given
at the time of purchase.

LAGNIAPPE: SONIC BRANDING

The sound of your brand is the logo that plays itself out in the mind of your guests. Sonic branding might be as important, if not more, than the logo you develop. Close your eyes and listen. More than likely, you will hear a tune or melody wafting from your television, phone, or YouTube. If successful, that tune will immediately make you think of a brand.

The clang you hear that tells you it's time for a story ripped from the headlines. Law & Order.

The drop of knowledge that introduces every Ted Talk.

The pop of a Snapple lid.

Ba...da..da..da..da... I'm loving it!

Sound has a unique way of connecting with consumers at a deep emotional level. As consumers continue to grow their dependence on voice, and as technology such as Amazon's Alexa or Google Home continues to become a more significant part of our lives, it becomes more important than ever for brands to create audio connections with consumers. Sonic branding can help build and reinforce your brand identity.

Senior Director of Marketing Strategy Trends & Insights at Viacom Sara Unger recently shared how sound is helping brands create connections. "In a world where we're constantly being assaulted by a flurry of sounds and images, the most memorable are often the most stripped down and simplified." As consumers, we have become more visual yet only partially attentive (catchy thoughts in 140 characters or less). Yet the power of sonic branding seems to be ever-present, though generally overlooked by many marketers.

Casinos have been at this sonic branding game for a while, and you probably did not even realize it. As the industry transitioned to coinless, operators quickly understood that the sound of coins falling into a tray was part of the experience real gamers looked for (or rather listened for). The guest needed to HEAR that they won. The sound of "winning" was quickly engineered into the machines. "We all need aural signals to create the emotional connection in our lives," says Audiobrain's Owner/Creative Director Audrey Arbeeny.

Sonic Branding Can Make You Feel a Certain Way

The *Harvard Business Review* has posed, "...the strategic use of sound can play an important role in positively differentiating a product or service, enhancing recall, creating preference, building trust, and even increasing sales."[15] Like a hit song, sonic branding can influence consumers in ways marketers want.

"...sound is housed in the emotional center of the brain; it is stored very deeply, which is why we respond to AND remember music and sound once it is stored."
— *Audrey Arbeeny*

Arbeeny, an Emmy Award-Winning executive producer, is a pioneer in the field of sonic branding.

In her work, she is guided by the notion that humans are deeply connected to sound. "We are natural receptors for sound and vibration," she says. "Our (adult) bodies are vibratory systems made of 50-68% percent water. Additionally, sound is housed in the emotional center of the brain; it is stored very deeply, which is why we respond to AND remember music and sound once it is stored. Think of a song from when you were a kid. You will remember every word even if you have not heard it in 30 years."

Jingle or Audio Logo?

We are all remarkably familiar with the use of a jingle to end a radio or television commercial – a short song that goes along with a brand.

While both jingles and audio logos are created to be in line with the brand's attributes, a jingle is typically designed to support a campaign and resonate in a short or medium term. An audio logo entails the creation of an entire language for the brand. This language is expressed across the entirety of the guest journey and is based on the brand promise and personality.

A great jingle can sometimes become a brand's audio logo. "I wish I were an Oscar Mayer Weiner," sings Arbeeny, "Jingles are just one touchpoint of sonic branding. An audio logo, or sonic logo, is a signature mark, like the NBC chimes or Intel inside sound. They, too, are a part of the sonic branding, more often used longer, and designed to be the iconic mark of the brand. Audio logos are intentionally aligned with the brand and strategically developed, while jingles are typically built as short-term assets that can sometimes become long-term equity."

Creating an Audio Logo

Think about the five notes that comprise the Intel mnemonic. Only five notes a total of three seconds, it has more than 20 musical sounds. The process of developing an audio logo can seem daunting, but it is something for which audio producers and (yes) agencies are well suited.

When Visa realized sound could make consumers feel safe and secure during their transactions, they released a distinctive sound which plays during digital and physical transactions. The sound signifying a secure, speedy transaction sparked a positive perception for the brand for about 83% of respondents!

Coca-Cola recently changed its sonic branding.

Even though the previous sonic landscape was able to carry their "Open Happiness" campaign, the marketing teams saw an opportunity to develop something that could tell the Coca-Cola story, from thirst to refreshment, through sound. The Taste the Feeling audio signature was developed to take the brand forward by relying on the drink itself. The new soundscape tells a story and evokes a visceral connection.

Think Avon is your mother's (or your grandmother's) cosmetic brand? Think again. The journey of Avon's sonic branding could be the journey your brand starts this year. Avon was a pioneer of sonic branding. Ask anyone who remembers the '50s or '60s, and they will remember the distinctive doorbell of "Avon calling." Before 2015 Avon was producing a little more than a dozen television spots per year and no digital content. By 2016, they had produced over 400 pieces of digital content. Does this sound familiar? Seeing the future of their communications identity, they recognized they needed to look beyond the visual to keep their brand relevant and integrated around the world. Avon saw an opportunity to create sonic brand touchpoints. The brand's musical journey began by showing pride in their history with the iconic chime. Then they gave the two-syllable name a woman's voice to music. The result is what they call the Avon Beauty Signature. This signature is modular and flexible, able to be integrated across all touchpoints. Within the first year, Avon integrated the audio signature across almost all internal and external communications across the globe. The signature was so successful, Avon developed it into a song that is being used and adapted in numerous global markets, further unifying their communications.

Skeet Hanks, founder of Lunar Baby Designs and longtime member of Southern rock band Beatin' Path, agrees with Unger. Having written music for the band and composed audio signatures for clients, he says, "The best approach — like creative design — is to keep it simple. The simplicity is what makes it 'singable' to anyone. You don't have to be a gifted singer to feel joy singing a simple tune. One of the main reasons branded tunes become iconic and memorable is because these brands were able to edit complexity out of the tunes."

Custom or License?

Investing in a custom audio signature helps ensure your brand does not get confused with another who might be licensing the same tune you are interested in. Sonic logos are just a few notes. So, it is important to strike the right ones. Signature Tones co-founder David Meerman Scott warns brand marketers from "borrowing" from the familiar. Some organizations "take songs that are familiar and just use them without permission."[16] This idea could result in numerous legal predicaments — even quite possibly land you in jail. Stock music is excellent. The problem is that everybody else – maybe even your biggest competitor – has the same music. If you are able to go the custom route, partner with someone who is going to take time to understand your brand and then compose something that is the perfect fit.

It is no surprise that Arbeeny also believes custom music is best. "Customizing the brand sound allows you to design it based on the brand attributes and create a solid foundation based on those values, mission statement, strategic goals, and desired guest experience," says Arbeeny.

You can then build upon that foundation. Eventually, you can include licensed music, say for an event or campaign, but now you will have criteria or a filter for the brand by which these one-off sounds are chosen. In addition, if you own your music, there will be no rights issues whatsoever. You can use it where and when you want. Another consideration is all the new mediums we currently have as they make it increasingly challenging and costly to use licensed commercial music.

Finding a Partner

If you are looking to develop a sonic branding system, look for a firm that specializes in sonic branding. Sonic branding agencies regularly work with ad agencies, as well as directly with clients. Arbeeny advises, "It's important for the sonic branding firm to become a part of an integrated team working on your audio assets."

She continues, "To ensure you actually are choosing a sonic branding agency, I would look at the deliverables and methodology: Is there research? Competitive analysis? Do they freelance their creative team or have them in-house? All of these are important factors in establishing sonic branding. They do not need to be a large firm, or one with global locations, but they need to immerse themselves in every part of the brand. There are several companies that refer to themselves as sonic branding firms, but the quality ones will have a formidable methodology. If the same company is willing to score your ad with no research or strategy preceding it, and plan to send you several demos first they may not be creating sonic branding, as I would see it. They are creating audio for a campaign."

Upfront research and strategy are necessary when choosing your sonic branding agency.

Be Prepared

Before you embark on this journey, there are some things to consider. Understand that you need to consider your sonic branding. Arbeeny agrees. "It is no longer a 'would like to,' 'maybe we can include' or a small optional line item. You can no longer say, 'I know a composer who has a garage band that can write something for us.' If you are not sonic branding now, you are falling behind the curve. The technological vehicles and smart devices, compounded with a sonically savvy audience, have made this imperative. The transparent presence across social media and new forms of brand communications means that brands that are not addressing this, not creating a cohesive tone and feel to their brand, may sound and feel outdated and out of touch with today's consumer."

If you are not sure where to start, you are not alone. Arbeeny continues, "We have brands that say, 'I really don't know how to do this, or what we need.' In some cases, these are large, global brands. Find and trust a partner that has the sonic branding expertise that can guide and get you there."

What You Can Do Today

Sonic branding, like branding in general, is about the experience. Casinos generally know the likes and dislikes of several of their guests. Why not have his/ her profile radio station playing when they arrive in their comped room. Did you know a sound chip on a room card can be customized? What is playing today on your shuttle — or your elevators —that articulates your casino and differentiates you from the competition. Arbeeny contends, "There are so many opportunities to connect with your audience right now. It is a fantastic time to be incorporating intentional audio, sonic branding, into the branding equation."

Every company can do this, even with the smallest of budgets. Create a sound logo. Make sure your call center has the right voice representing your brand. Little by little, form your cohesive brand sound. It is more important than ever to understand how music and sound play a role in your communications.

ACKNOWLEDGEMENT

The years I've spent writing on the topic of casino marketing and casino branding have been more fulfilling than I would have ever expected.

The support of friends, family and associates was invaluable. I have been blessed with some who provided so much consistent support that the word "invaluable" seems so small.

Elissa Plastino has been my proofer extraordinaire with this project and many more. I can't thank you enough for those days when you find the perfect word I can't seem to reach.

James "Skeet" Hanks has been a friend for longer than anyone else involved in this project. His perspective and creative genius is beyond measure.

I am sure Scott Oeschger never expected to be my sounding board, yet here he is - still helping me find my groove.

Jan Talamo took my words and thoughts and coined the term "Jules Rules".

Denise Lee Yohn, who without knowing it, has inspired almost all of chapter 3. She really did "write the book" on the topic of operationalization of your brand.

Louis Toscano braved the world of putting his passion onto a written page and set an example for me to follow.

Finally, I tip my hat to all the brand marketers that have not only taught and inspired me, but also let me spread my branding wings to places even I didn't know I could go.

ABOUT THE AUTHOR

Julia Carcamo

 Born and raised in New Orleans, Julia began her career in what was the newly burgeoning Gulf South gaming market. Subsequently she moved to Las Vegas to serve as Director of Brand Marketing for Caesars Entertainment (Harrah's), developing the brand architecture for the company's core brands, including Harrah's overall corporate brand positioning and the refinement of the industry's paragon loyalty program, Total Rewards®.

Always up for a challenge, Julia answered a call from Wynn Resorts to develop branding for the company's signature properties as well as its various stores and restaurants.

She was at the helm of development of the Isle of Capri house of brands, introducing new brands and successfully connecting with new and inactive guests, and the reintroduction of the iconic Lady

Luck Casino brand. Recognizing the impact the Hispanic market is having, she has co-founded espÑOLA – a Hispanic marketing and engagement agency.

Today, Julia serves as president and chief brand strategist at J Carcamo & Associates, serving casino properties from coast to coast. She writes on a variety of casino and general marketing topics and is the founder of the highly lauded Casino Marketing Boot Camp.